AF327176

Arundel Books
$12.00
Mazzotti, /Sakra Boccata
Poetry/Floor
Trade Paperback
00516997

ISBN 978-1-937027-16-2
First Edition, First Printing
Ugly Duckling Presse
232 Third Street, #E303, Brooklyn, NY 11215
uglyducklingpresse.org

Distributed by SPD/Small Press Distribution
1341 Seventh Street, Berkeley, CA 94710
spdbooks.org

Some of these translations were first published in 2012 in *Cerisse Press Vol. 2, n. 9, Asymptote, Poems and Poetics, Nomadics, The Broome Street Review*, and *Catch Up*.

Cover design by Mary Anne Carter
Typeset by Carly Dashiell in Minion and Comfortaa
Books printed on recycled paper
and bound at McNaughton & Gunn

This book has been partially funded by the Dean of Academic Affairs in the School of Arts and Sciences at Tufts University. Additional support for this publication was provided by the National Endowment for the Arts.

José Antonio Mazzotti

SAKRA BOCCATA

Translation by Clayton Eshleman

Prologue by Raúl Zurita

To the Reader: a few notes appear at the end of this book
that may help explain the meaning of the title and some lines
marked with an asterisk (*) in the poems.

EROS AND THE SACRED: THE SAKRA BOCCATA OF JOSÉ ANTONIO MAZZOTTI

José Antonio Mazzotti's *Sakra Boccata* is a book that in its brief sequence of twenty-eight poems—the number in a lunar cycle—displays one of the most revelatory poetries in contemporary Latin America. These poems enter into a dialogue with the grand saga of the literature of passion and with the multiple topoi and crossroads displayed by the theme of love in its affirmations and negations since the *Song of Songs*, on the one hand, and Sappho's fragments, on the other, over twenty-five hundred years of writing.

As part of this vast cycle, Mazzotti's poems create a sort of polyphony that touches on the most direct and varied forms of erotic love. They explore the nuances, subtleties, edges, and folds of a real language, spoken and practiced in one region, a language that will be charged, after the inevitable separation of lovers, to re-unite them via the exorcism of writing. Thus the title of the book, *Sakra Boccata*, alludes in part to the realm of the sacred in the era of a dissident orthography typical of end-of the-century and new-millenium Peruvian poetry (because of Sakra). At the same time because of Boccatta which in Italian means "mouthful" (Mazzotti comes from an ancient Milanese family) it seeks to secure the immediacy of oral language in writing. The language of Mazzotti's poems identifies a specific speech at one moment of the evolution of Spanish, in particular Peruvian Spanish. For this reason, since it is an erotic speech as well, it concretizes a vision that seems to come from the depths of the language of the flesh and its desire to devour and to be devoured by the other in an extreme realization of a merger with the beloved.

Thus this poetry refers to oral ingestion and expulsion as a symbol of knowledge, confronting and at the same time affirming the famous disintegration of the lover and of lovers in Lucretius's *On the Nature of Things*, in which the author compares the consumption of food and drink that are incorporated into our being with the impossibility of such in the case of lovers[*]. What the mouth swallows is what the body ends up assimilating and thereby incorporating as part of its own essence. In contrast with Lucretius (and with all literature of isolation), but like the *Song of Songs* and all the mystic poetry derived from the *Song*, the lover in *Sakra Boccata* affirms his desire to devour, to ingest the beloved body in order to merge with it entirely.

Beyond any recent psychoanalytical interpretation, these poems display a carnal, erotic version of the never exhausted Neo-Platonic theme of perfect love achieved by two beings to erase all the physical and mental distance between them. The myth of the androgyne, of the better half, of the middle and lost Paradise are reactivated in this poetry that magisterially combines multiple rhythms, some rapid and panting (as is proper to passion), and some with a slow and reflective pulse (as times of rest and uncertainty). Mazzotti's poetry achieves the extraordinary materialization of this theme through the display of a language that never becomes abstract but instead always names real scenes, presenting us with a merger not only of bodies searching for each other but of language itself with the words that constitute it, as if the poems would like to devour themselves in a grand sexual act in which culture, eroticism and nature would once and for all erase their borders:

> Vusco volver Vallejo vibra yo también pero saliendo de un
> >laberinto de hielo
> Vusco tu rosca hosca y colorada tus pantuflas invisibles el reflejo
> >de un árbol sobre el lago
>
> I vie to revert Vallejo vibrates I too but getting out of an ice
> >labyrinth
> I vie with your sullen and ruddy bun your invisible
> >slippers a tree's reflection in the lake

---

[*] This chapter appears in Book IV of the cited text. I quote a fragment: *The food solids, the drink / that allow us to remain alive / occupy fixed places in our bodies / once they have been ingested, and thus it is easy to satisfy the desire to eat and drink. / But from a beautiful face, from a soft skin, nothing remains in our body, nothing / can enter us, except images / impalpable and vain simulacra, / despicable hope that very quickly vanishes.*

This destructive dimension of desire also merges with the memory of or yearning for purity that confers on Mazzotti's poems a multidimensionality seldom to be found in poetry focused on the theme of love. On one hand, Mazzotti's is a poetry of language, where the Spanish turns over on itself to sound in a new way, unheard of before. On the other hand, it is a situated poetry, Peruvian, a poetry that cannot stop being Peruvian in as much as Peruvian poetry makes up one of the most powerful currents in writings from the diverse regions of the Spanish language.

José Antonio Mazzotti has expanded the notions that we as readers might have concerning eroticism, love, and the immemorial yearning to merge with what we love, which is ultimately the longing of all poetry. This brief sequence of poems makes that yearning immediately visible in the rich and difficult range of erotic and mystical writing in the "lengua casta-i-llana" ("tongue chaste-and-plain"), as the dedication of this book states. But such a tongue concerns the concrete lives, sufferings and dreams that have been searching in it for the love, peace and simplicity they have not found for over five hundred years. *Sakra Boccata* is an advance on that potential encounter and on that impetuous merger with the world that we seek and adore. The irruption of these twenty-eight poems and their dream in our awake world is a triumph for poetry, but beyond anything that can be said it is a triumph for our bodies. For our South American bodies so often devoured by everything and anyone, except by love.

— Raúl Zurita

Santiago de Chile, July, 2006

*A los amantes de la lengua
casta-i-llana*

*To the lovers of the tongue
chaste-and-plain* [*]

La Luna, de puro nueva, se arroja sobre el Sol. Miren su cabellera
        incendiando el firmamento. Su piel curtida y blanca como la
        noche.

Una espalda cubre una barba. Un chorro de alga se mezcla con la
        lengua.
Han descendido al fondo de los mares sobre un primer piso.

En la ciudad los guardianes pasean centinelas de su sueño. Un
        secreto de a dos es un milagro
De los libres, esos astros que se cruzan en las autopistas y por un
        instante apenas
Se miran lo que duran los cometas.

Te soñé todas las noches por más de 300 años, contaba las sortijas del
        rosario hasta quedar dormido
Y ensartaba su Círculo Perfecto con la aguja de tu órbita.

Aries se deja arrastrar por la fuerza del Sol
A los mayores arrecifes de la costa:

Y las olas martillean Tu Nombre, chorreando por la espuma el néctar
        duraznero de tu Sakra Herida,
La alegría de las catacumbas, la resurrección de los muertos
Y la Vida Eterna.

1

The Moon, completely new, rushes over the Sun. Look at her head of
     hair setting the firmament on fire. Her skin hardened and white
     like the night.

A back covers a beard. A gush of seaweed mixes with the tongue.
They have descended to the bottom of the seas on the first floor.

In the city guardians stroll by, sentries of their dream. The secret of
     two is a miracle
Of the free, those heavenly bodies who pass each other on the
     highways and for barely an instant
Look at each other as lastingly as comets.

I dreamed about you every night for more than 300 years, I counted
     rosary beads until falling asleep
And threaded their Perfect Circle with the needle of your orbit.

Aries allows himself to be dragged by the Sun's power
To the greatest reefs of the coast:

And the waves hammer Your Name, gushing through the foam the
     peach tree nectar of your Sakra Wound,
The happiness of the catacombs, the resurrection of the dead
And Life Eternal

2

Llueve sobre los montes de Cibelia
Alucina la Luna su respaldo de nubes
Pero las que se acercan son de humo
Nubes de fusinas y de bombardeos
Allí donde Luna decidió acampar por unos días
Largos como dos embarcaderos
Y pasea la marea dócilmente fisgoneando las ventanas
De las muchachas febles
Y a cada una le irradia la pequeñez del cuerpo
Y el esplendor de su olor de tamarindo
Cada árbol de carne es un marisco estirado
Arrastra su pelambre por las veredas lavadas
Sus labios infinitos besando la tierra
Su caracol levantado como una gota de miel
Bifronte y consistente
Allí Luna desciende de los aires
Para posar su planta
Quema su huella en la punta de los lapiceros
La ciudad se enrojece ante su nombre
Ha llegado la diosa ambarina
El mar explosiona sobre el risco nocturno:

Llueve sobre los montes de Cibelia

2

It rains on the mountains of Cibelia
The Moon hallucinates her backing of clouds
But those that draw near are made of smoke
Clouds of factories and of bombardments
There where Moon decides to encamp for a few days
As long as two piers
And docilely the tide strolls by snooping on the windows
Of feeble girls
And irradiates for each one the smallness of her body
And the splendor of her tamarind odor
Each tree of flesh is a stretched shellfish
She drags her mop of hair across the washed sidewalks
Her infinite lips kissing the ground
Her snail raised like a drop of honey
Bifrontal and consistent
There Moon descends through the air
In order to plant her sole
She burns her footprint onto the tip of the pens
The city blushes in the presence of her name
The amber goddess has arrived [*]
The sea explodes over the nocturnal cliff

It rains on the mountains of Cibelia

3

Tu Koncha es el lugar exquisito más dentro de la Guerra
Allí hay que llegar con la destreza del piloto herido
Manejar los laberintos como la palma de su mano
Seguir cada curva como el mapa de un tesoro
Con sus paredes y sus puertas
Gritando Ron Rojo Ron Rojo / Nunca Destrucción
Desgarramiento de cuerpos sólo existe el que desbroza
Tus vellos recortados ante el espejo feliz
Ojo inmenso de la cerradura del delirio que te observa
Mira el rosado de su pliegue
Como el labio que cubre el horizonte
Al levantar la niebla

Tu Koncha es el espacio al centro de la Cruz del Sur
Santifica la ciudad con su rayo
Todos sus pecados se transforman en guirnaldas
Rodeando a la Virgen de Chapi con su manto negro
El olor del incienso trae brisa de espuma
Levita sobre los huesos
Besa la Vara del Señor y el oro se desliza de su frente
Ojos más verdes que el fondo de la selva
Purifica el orín de todas las paredes
Ventila el dedo la boca inferior
Repta la lengua por la acequia perfumada

Tu Koncha es ese músculo esponjoso que late
Y no deja de latir

3

Your Konch is that exquisite place most deeply inside the War [*]
One must arrive there with the dexterity of the wounded pilot
Navigating labyrinths like the palm of his hand
Following each curve like a treasure map
With its walls and its gates
Shouting Red Rum Red Rum / Destruction Never [*]
Only the rending of bodies exists that of the clearing of
Your down trimmed before the happy mirror
Immense eye of the delirious lock that observes you
You regard the pink of its pleat
Like the lip that covers the horizon
As the fog lifts

Your Konch is the space at the center of the Southern Cross
It sanctifies the city with its ray
All sins are transformed into garlands
Surrounding the Virgin of Chapi in her black mantle [*]
The aroma of incense brings a foaming breeze
It levitates over the bones
It kisses the Lord's Staff and the gold slips from her forehead
Eyes more verdant than the forest's depths
It purifies the urine on all the walls
The finger ventilates the lower mouth
The tongue snakes across the perfumed gutter

Your Konch is that throbbing spongy muscle
That never stops throbbing

Vusco volver Vallejo vibra yo también pero saliendo de un laberinto
    de hielo
Vusco tu rosca hosca y colorada tus pantuflas invisibles el reflejo de
    un árbol sobre el lago
En ellos se concentra tu perfil de Lemnia de lunática marea de control
Andrónico los navegantes de ese lago no reconocerán sus estrellas así
    dicen
Tiemblan como el niño que se acerca a su primer acto de amor
Se llamaba Yola y él tenía quince años las olas arañaban los cirros el
    Círculo Negro dio
Su vuelta primera y el muchacho se lanzó a la Resurrección
De la Carne porque Santo es el Nombre del Señor
Que habita entre tus Rocas Cianeas has vuelto de la Nada como un
    sueño recordado
Tras siglos de silencio Santo es el Nombre
Del Señor porque cura las heridas alivia a los enfermos nos bendice
Con su carne en dos ríos concéntricos boca
Del claro día que conjuga
Bajo los dobles arcos de su sangre, por donde
Hay que pasar tan de puntillas

Vusco Vusco Vusco Vusco
Tu rosca hosca y colorada tus pantuflas invisibles el reflejo de un árbol
Sobre el lago

4

I vie to revert Vallejo vibrates I too but getting out of an ice labyrinth *
I vie with your sullen and ruddy bun your invisible slippers a tree's
    reflection in the lake
In these is concentrated your Lemnian profile of a lunatic tide of
    Andronican *
Control the navigators of that lake do not recognize its stars so they say
They tremble like the child approaching his first act of love
Her name was Yola and he was fifteen the waves were scraping the
    cirruses the Black Circle made
Its first turn and the boy threw himself at the Resurrection
Of the Flesh because Blessed is the Name of the Lord
Who dwells between your Cyanean Rocks you've returned from
    Nothing like a remembered dream *
After centuries of silence Blessed is the Name
Of the Lord because he heals wounds comforts the sick blesses us
With his flesh in two concentric rivers mouth
Of the bright day that conjugates *
Under the double arches of your blood, where
One can only pass on tiptoes *

I vie I vie I vie I vie
Your sullen and ruddy bun your invisible slippers a tree's reflection
In the lake

5

Porque bendita Tú eres entre todas las mujeres
Y bendito ese bulto carnoso como un escaramujo
Salva mi alma con la Transustanciación de la Carne
En Vino y Pan de Gloria en este altar me sacrifico
Doy de comer a mi diosa como a un monstruo marino
Beso las dos mejillas de su Rostro
Santa Madrina Madre del Vicio
Entrégate a nosotros los pecadores
Repártenos el pez a discreción
                              Danos tu paz
Porque bendita Tú eres
Entre todas las mujeres
Y bendito es el fruto
Del zumo blanco y del zumo
Transparente

5

Because blessed You are among all women
And blessed this fleshy bulk like a dog rose
It saves my soul with the Transubstantiation of the Flesh
In Wine and Bread of the Glory on this altar I sacrifice myself
I feed my goddess as if she were a sea monster
I kiss the two cheeks of her Face
Saintly Godmother Mother of Vice
Surrender to us the sinners
Deliver the fish as you choose
                              Give us your peace

Because You are blessed
Among all women
And blessed is the fruit
Of the white juice and of the transparent
Juice

*Eu canto assim
como que eu choro*

— Bandeira

Choro todas las noches cuando las fogatas aúllan y no pasan las aves
     por encima
Choro porque este chanto es más dulce que la melodía de los cardenales
A la hora del Sancto
Sanctorum las delicias de las yemas
Se derriten en la boca
La música repta
Con la fuerza de los caparazones
Choro limpio y prolongado se abre a escondidas
Su aroma de sándalo su dulce
De limonada
Asienta las espaldas sobre el nácar
Permite contemplar la perfección de sus líneas
Pequeña criatura engendro de mamífero
En la ínfima prisa de los siglos
Choro celeste y blanco como el aire sobre el Polo
Su reino de hielo desgajado viaja por el océano
Se mezcla con los glaciares
Desata su lluvia densa cuando el Sol lo toca
Choro que moja las dunas y desembarca
A declarar la Independencia
Choro perdido en una noche de domingo
Sin Padre sobre el mundo
Choro como un niño abandonado a la hora de los diablos
Choro que nutres hasta la última papila

6

*I sing exactly
like I cry*

— Bandeira

Mussel every night when the bonfires howl and birds do not fly
     overhead
Mussel because this mounting is sweeter than a cardinal's melody *
At the hour of the Holy of
Holies the delights of the fingertips
Are dissolved in the mouth
The music crawls
With the strength of caparisons
Mussel clean and oblong secretly opening
Its aroma of sandalwood its sweetness
Of lemonade
It places its back on the nacre
Enabling the perfection of its lines to be contemplated
A little creature a mammal fetus
In the abject speed of the centuries
Mussel sky-blue and white like the air over the Pole
Its kingdom of broken up ice travels through the ocean
Mixing with glaciers
Unleashing dense rain when touched by the Sun
Mussel that moistens the dunes and disembarks
In order to declare Independence
Mussel lost one Sunday night
Without a Father in the world
Mussel like an abandoned child at the satanic hour
Mussel that nourishes even the last papilla

7

Estás triste LoKilla me dices porque el Reino se levanta
Los bárbaros se mueven por la costa norte
Al sur los senadores exigen privilegios
Y cuestionan en el Foro la Majestad de tu frente
Olvidan los tontos que Tú reinas por la misma libertad
Que les diste de existir y de moverse por la urbe
De soñar con praderas y con lagos que sus pies jamás pisaron
De tocar con sus ojos las estrellas que les marcan el camino
Y ahora te quieren presa
Y a su servicio
Y arrancan de tus alas esas plumas que les sirven
Para inflamar infundios

Oh LoKilla Reina mía Reina
De todos los bienaventurados
Y de los pobres que aceptamos tus palabras
Como el pan bendito
Estaremos a tu lado hasta la Muerte
Tu Imperio es nuestra Salvación
De Ti sube la columna que sostiene las constelaciones
Y en ellas leemos nuestros versos
Que alaban la gloria de tu poderío
La belleza que excede todo ojo y toda lengua
La dulcísima caverna donde el mundo nace
Y donde toda pena se consuela
Con tu sabor de vino

7

You tell me you are sad LittleKrazyOne because the Kingdom is in
    revolt *
Barbarians move along the northern coast
In the south the senators are demanding special deals
And in the Forum they question the Majesty of your forehead
These fools forget that You reign with the same freedom
That you gave them to exist and to move through the metropolis
To dream of meadows and lakes their feet have never tread
To touch with their eyes the stars that mark the path
And now they want you as a prisoner
And at their service
And they tear out your wings those feathers they use
To stir up lies

Oh LittleKrazyOne Queen my Queen
Of all the beatified
And of the poor who accept your words
Like consecrated bread
We'll remain at your side unto Death
Your Empire is our Salvation
From You rises the column that supports the constellations
And on them we read our poems
That extol the glory of your power
The beauty that surpasses every eye and every tongue
The sweetest cavern in which the world is born
And where all grief is consoled
With your vinous flavor

La inclinación de la onda se persigue a sí misma. Esa dilatación
Revuelve las profundidades y se posa en una duna
En mira exacta hacia la superficie esperando el momento añorado
Cuando el Sol se apaga en interregno de la Luna
En plena luz del día y cantan algas y caparazones
La carne del océano descansa de sus cuchillos
Es la hora en que los peces tragan su propio cuidado
Palpitando en el Caos
Luna de Escorpio en la punta del lanzón
La inclinación de la onda se levanta
Erige su mano de espuma intentando tocarlos
Es la hora en que la playa rechina de sardinas
Que alimentan el árbol
Que tarde o temprano volverá a las aguas
Para posarse en la duna más dorada
Chorreando de luz

8

The slope of the wave pursues itself. This dilation
Stirs the depths and settles on a dune
Its sight fixed on the surface awaiting the longed for moment
When the Sun goes out in an interregnum with the Moon
In broad daylight and seaweed and caparisons sing
And the flesh of the ocean rests from its knives
It's the hour in which fish swallow their own anxiety
Throbbing in Chaos
Moon of Scorpio on the lance point
The slope of the wave rises
Raises up its foaming hand intending to touch them
It's the hour in which the beach creaks with sardines
Which nurture the tree
Which sooner or later will return to the waters
To settle on the most golden dune
Gushing light

9

Te amo con la locura del pie atrapado bajo la quilla
Te amo con la prisa del que siente pasos en la puerta
Y arriesga la altura para no ser capturado
Te amo parado y en la tina y bajo todos los nogales
Y en la blandura espesa de la nieve
Y en la silla del pupitre cuando las luces se apagan
Y proclamo la victoria
De tu Fosa Todopoderosa
Loado sea el Nombre del Señor bajo su altura
Los círculos perfectos como andenes de Moray
Una gota cayendo eternamente sobre la superficie
Expandiendo sus ondas mientras los planetas
Se alínean en la curva de su canto
Rosa pulposa de todos los señoríos
Boquita de caramelo cutis de seda
En la culposa oscuridad del infinito

Te amo como si fuera esta noche
La primera vez

9

I love you with the madness of a foot caught under the keel
I love you with the speed of one sensing footsteps at the door
Who risks the heights to avoid capture
I love you standing and in the bathtub and under every walnut tree
And in the heavy softness of the snow
And in the desk chair when the lights go out
And I proclaim the victory
Of the Almighty Deep
Praised be the Name of the Lord under his height
Perfect circles like Moray's Incan terraces
A drop eternally falling onto the surface
Extending its waves while the planets
Line up on the curve of its song
Fleshy rose of all the seigneuries
Little caramel mouth silken cutis [*]
In the culpable darkness of the infinite

I love you as if this night were
The first time

La soledad del espejo no se resarce de su espera
Como el Túnel del Tiempo es una trompa que traga cuanta carne
Se ofrezca para el sacrificio es una trompa
Viscosa y bienoliente de sudores anteriores
Pintada de cuerpos dorados cobra su propia vida
Recuerda ciudades laberintos
Al borde de un río de barro
Airea el final del verano y busca almejas
Al canto de un abismo seco
Sus pasos lo conducen por iglesias
Erguidas en pezones y en su puerta desciende
Al bosque de los huesos centenarios
Tanta muerte y no poder nada contra la vida
Cambia el espejo de colores
Alumbra desde la puerta el manto púrpura
De la Virgen de la Candelaria
Oh Santa María Madre de Dios ampara a tus corderitos
Que quieren perpetuarse en el espejo
Oh Santa María Madre de Dios
Tú misma
Que con el Espíritu Santo
Resplandeciste una noche ante el caldero
De cobre

10

The solitude of the mirror does not recoup its expectations
Like the Tunnel of Time it's a trunk that swallows whatever meat
It offers itself as a sacrifice it's a trunk
Viscous and fragrant with sweat from the past
Painted with golden bodies it recovers its own life
It remembers labyrinthine cities
On the bank of a muddy river
It ventilates the end of summer and searches for clams
At the edge of a dry abyss
Its steps lead it through churches
Erect as nipples and at their doors it descends
Into the woods of the centenary bones
So much death and no power at all against life *
The mirror changes colors
It illuminates from the doorway the purple mantle
Of the Virgin of Candlemas
Oh Saint Mary Mother of God shelter your little lambs
Who seek to perpetuate themselves in the mirror
Oh Saint Mary Mother of God
You yourself
Who with the Holy Ghost
Gleamed one night before the copper
Cauldron

Recuperamos nuestra inocencia perdida
El sabor del vino se convierte en paladar
Otrora espíritus del corpus divino
Vivían juntos y revueltos anverso y reverso
Andrógino perfecto apto para sí mismo
Doble gozo doble erizamiento
Pasado y futuro concentrados y el presente
Abierto como un arca infinita
Si no sabes lo que quieres no lo conseguirás
Hay eclipse de luna sobre el lomo de Escorpio
Señalan los astrólogos la conveniencia del ciclo
Busca dentro de ti busca al fondo
Encontrarás la bolsa de cuero en que flotaban
Por delante la cara del macho y la hembra en la nuca
O al revés se tocaban estirando la mano
Pensaban al unísono
Estas palabras lluviosas de las que asciende
Un humo azul

Habemus Papam

11

We regain our lost innocence
The wine's flavor is converted on the palate
Spirits formerly of the divine body
Live joined and jumbled obverse and reverse
A perfect androgyne self-sufficient
Double joy double bristling
The past and the future concentrated and the present
Open like an infinite arc
If you don't know what you're after you'll never get it
There's a lunar eclipse on the back of Scorpio
The astrologers point out the harmony of the cycle
Look within yourself look deep
You'll find the leather bag in which the male's face
And the female's nape float up front
Or inside out they touch each other stretching forth their hands
They were pondering in unison
These rainy words out of which a blue smoke
Ascends

Habemus Papam

Brilla la página en blanco apagando el silencio de la tarde
Respira de pronto un cartílago de vértebra dibuja
El lomo de un monstruo en el lago
Entrando y saliendo
Lleva en la cresta espinas y un hilillo de sangre
Penetra sus dos mejillas y los ojos de fuego
Hilvanan su ritmo transparente
Busca en el agua el alimento imposible
Piensa que un día lo tuvo eran las diez de la mañana
Los autos se alejaban allá abajo en la calle
Campanas de la iglesia rodeaban el encuentro
Del dulce gemido de escamas penetradas
El pez glorificado entre los sables del marino
Adicto al agua dulce y condenado
A la cumbre de las olas
Ahora repta
Por esta arena
Entrando y saliendo
Del fondo del lago

12

The page shining blankly extinguishes the evening's silence
Breathing suddenly a vertebral cartilage outlines
The back of a monster in the lake
Surfacing and descending
It has a spiny crest and a trickle of blood
Penetrates its two cheeks and its fiery eyes
Baste its transparent rhythm
It searches in the water for impossible nourishment
Thinking that the last time it had some it was 10 A.M.
The cars down there in the street were moving away
Church bells were encircling the meeting
Of sweet moans in penetrated scales
The fish glorified between the sailor's sabers
Fond of fresh water and condemned
To the crest of the waves
Now crawls
Along this sand
Descending and surfacing
From the bottom of the lake

13

Ah late molúsculo de plata sigue tu camino
Animalito de Dios dijo Fray Gómez
El viejo se las sabe todas cuentan
Hoy nos encerró en su celda
Olía a rosas y alquitrán
Pero hicimos el amor como las liendres
Y en nombre del Señor nos perdonó
Desde entonces soy santo
Pero no como San Tiváñez
Sino como el Iluminado
Que escribe bajo la Luna y bota saliva
Dejando las uñas en los tallos
El traje en casa
Molúsculo dorado
Repta por los riachuelos
Escapa en las madrugadas
Porque cura la locura y vuelve cura
Que aprende a hacer milagros
Con su pincel de Orfeo

Y escribo escribo escribo
Como el preso que marca las paredes
Para contar los días

13

Ah throb silver molluscle follow your road *
God's little animal said Friar Gómez *
The old man knows everything they say
Today he locked us up in his cell
It smelled of roses and tar
But we made love like two nits
And in the name of the Lord he pardoned us
Since then I am a saint
Not like Saint Tiváñez *
But like the Enlightened one
Who writes under the Moon and wastes saliva
Leaving his fingernails on the stalks
His clothes at home
Golden molluscle
Crawl through the brooks
Escape at dawn
Because it cures madness and turns you into a priest
Who learns how to perform miracles
With Orpheus's paintbrush

And I write I write I write
Like the prisoner marking the walls
So as to count the days

14

Si los muertos felices se transforman en estrellas
Y el cúmulo del tiempo es torre que los toca ahí vamos llegando
Qué son dos andróginos corriendo perseguidos por el bosque
Sin Sol que ilumine la caída de la noche
Sino sólo el sinnúmero de pasos para rencontrarse
Ahora despliegan un código secreto los caninos
Asedian y es prudente camuflarse en el follaje
Dejando que pasen las hordas por encima de sus cabezas
Hiriendo las cavernas con su Dedo de Fuego
Los muertos se levantan los pajaritos
Abrelatas escinden las paredes
Guiando al molúsculo sabroso con torsión de tiro
Como si la vida se hubieran esperado
Morirán como todos algún día
Del cual no les queda ni el recuerdo
Ahora que iluminan desde el cielo
Otro sendero de plata
Por los pinos

14

If the happy dead transform themselves into stars
And the accumulation of time is a tower that touches them there
    while we arrive
Who are those two androgynes running pursued through the woods
With no Sun to illuminate nightfall
But only endless footsteps to re-encounter themselves
Now they are unfolding a secret codex the canines
Besiege and it's prudent to camouflage with foliage
Letting the hordes pass overhead
Wounding the caverns with their Finger of Fire
The dead rise the little can-opener
Birds divide the walls
Guiding the tasty molluscle with a rotary shot
As if in life they had been waiting
They will die like everybody else on a day
They do not even remember
Now that from the sky they illuminate
Another silver path
Through the pines

¿Qué dicen los muertos desde su eternidad?
¿Pensarán con los huesos que han dejado por la tierra
Sembrados como tallos para recordarnos
Que pronto no seremos más que amebas
Y todo lo querido se disuelve como polvo en el agua
Como polvo en el viento
En el camino?

¿Qué dicen cuando dos que se buscan al final se encuentran
Y escupen la solemnidad de su reino?
¿Se vengan sutilmente separándolos
Tendiéndoles trampas como si fueran perros
Sin pensamiento sin vergüenza?
¿O simplemente les apagan las luces
y lanzan sus aviones en distancias opuestas?

¿Qué dicen? ¿Qué decimos?

15

What do the dead say from their eternity?
Might they be thinking with the bones they've left on earth
Planted like stalks to remind us
That soon we'll be no more than amoebas
And that all we have loved will dissolve like dust in water
Like dust in the wind
Down the road?

What do they say when two looking for each other find each other
        in the end
And spit on the solemnity of their kingdom?
Will the dead take revenge subtly separating them
Setting traps for them as if they were dogs
Without minds without shame?
Or simply do they turn out the lights
And launch their airplanes in opposite directions?

What do they say? What do we say?

Hay un pozo de hielo sobre el asfalto rajado
Hay un pino radiante cosquilleando al Sol
Hay una tarde de martes que se duerme en la ciudad
Sobre todos los limbos sobre todos los tambos sobre todos
Los rumbos
Y no asoman tus ojos
Como una estampilla ilegible como un timbre sordo
El planeta un trompo ebrio
Pregunta por los pedazos
Cantando sus fonemas
Circulares
Y baja el solsticio hasta el lugar más austral
Más cerca de ti siempre pero desde lejos
A coronar mi sombra
A bendecirme con Su rayo larguísimo de fuego
Su cabellera que pasea como una carroza
Por los siglos de los siglos

Amén

16

There is a puddle of ice on the cracked asphalt
There is a radiant pine tickling the Sun
There is a Tuesday afternoon falling asleep in the city
On all the limbos on all the inns on all
The directions
And your eyes do not appear
Like an illegible stamp like a mute doorbell
The planet like a drunkenly spinning top .
Asks for fragments
Singing its circular
Phonemes
And the solstice descends to the most southern spot
Closer to you always but still distant
To crown my shadow
To bless me with Its longest fiery ray
Its head of hair passing like a carriage
Forever and ever

Amen

Porque eres Madre de todos los mortales
Y hasta apareces en las paredes de Chicago
Aquí en este tu día una flor muy negra
Más negra que tu cola cabellera
Se esparce con los pétalos mojados
Busca su longitud por las alturas
Se enreda en los ramales y como el adorno
De la primera Navidad prende sus lucecitas

Porque has venido

Y los pájaros estiran el pescuezo
Tarareando la gloria de Tu Nombre
La indiscutible santidad de tus sandalias
Tu boca bendita tu saliva
De piscina amniótica

Because you are Mother of all mortals
And appear even on Chicago walls
Here on this your day a flower very black
Blacker than your head of hair tail
Scatters its moist petals
Seeking its length by the heights
It gets caught up in branches and like a decoration
From the first Christmas turns on its tiny lights

Because you have come

And the birds stretched forth their necks
Humming the glory of your Name
The indisputable sanctity of your sandals
Your blessed mouth the saliva
Of your amniotic piscine

¿Por qué desaparece el poeta de la faz de la tierra
Como si se hundiera
Y ganan las elecciones los soldados los mejores sueldos birladores
Que esconden sus denarios detrás de cada sílaba por qué desaparecen
Las nubes protectoras y el Sol nos latiguea sin cubrirse
Hace siglos del globo de la Luna?

He bajado a los Infiernos para rescatarte y llevo las manos heridas
Los extraños precipicios centellean
Y salen enanos orejudos de las cuevas preguntando
Cartones y documentos sayón de costal y sólo una flauta en la mano
La misión del peregrino siempre será secreta pues a ti sólo te concierne
Tú que te casaste con tantos martilleros que ocupaste
Un trono de lava y las plumas quemadas
Ave María Santísima Pagana te mereces el Reino de la Tierra
Tu molúsculo de diosa vivirá en mis cantos y aunque mis pecados
Te envíen al Reino de las Sombras volverás
Como el castaño que se incendia cada otoño
Y deja sus botones enterrados

¿Por qué desaparece el poeta si no es para traerte
limpiando la hojarasca aún helada
para alumbrar los atajos
en que tus pies marcarán una a una las piedras
como tus dientes en la espalda?

El Infierno, Euridice, es tu ausencia
Sobre la faz de la tierra

18

Why does the poet disappear from the face of the earth
As if he would sink
And soldiers win the elections swindlers the best salaries
Hiding their denari behind each syllable why do the protective clouds
Disappear and the Sun flog us without covering itself
For centuries with the lunar globe?

I have descended to Hades to rescue you and I bear wounded hands
Strange chasms sparkle
And big-eared dwarfs emerge from caves asking for
Cardboard and documents sackcloth and only a flute in hand
The pilgrim's mission will always be secret because it only concerns you
You who have married so many auctioneers who have occupied
A throne of lava and burnt plumes
Ave Maria Most Saintly Pagan you deserve the Kingdom of the Earth
Your goddess molluscle will live in my songs and even if my sins
Send you to the Kingdom of Shadows you will return
Like the chestnut tree that catches fire each autumn
And leaves its buds buried

Why does the poet disappear if not to retrieve you
Clearing the still frozen dead leaves
In order to light up the shortcuts
Where your feet mark one by one the stones
Like your teeth in my back?

Hades, Eurydice, is your absence
On the face of the earth

Suena el verano como trompa alegre porque el huracán se asolapa
Lleva tu nombre la primera letra la que contiene
Colinas y forados intangibles
Paredes color ladrillo
Origen de la carne primordiaca
Todos los nombres derivan de ese ojo
Las tangentes y las convergentes
Los remolinos que bajan por leguas a estrellarse
Chupan la piel de los paisajes
Todo vuelve a su antigua habitación
Como en el caos y confusión primera

Summer sounds like a lively horn because the hurricane is overlapped
It bears your name the first letter the one that contains
Hills and intangible openings
Brick-colored walls
The origin of primordiac flesh [*]
All names derive from this eye
Tangents and convergents
Whirlpools descending league-wise to burst
They suck at the landscapes' skin
All returns to its ancient habitation
As in chaos and the first confusion [*]

20

Lo huelo lo escudriño lo medito
Lo busco lo despeino lo revuelvo
Lo saco de la almohada lo persigo
Lo hinco lo ataranto lo respeto
Lo peso lo evalúo lo distingo
Lo aplaudo lo alecciono lo entusiasmo
Lo miro lo espejeo lo palpito
Lo salo lo penetro lo digiero
Lo estrujo lo atornillo lo lastimo
Lo escucho lo sujeto lo consuelo
Lo raspo lo humedezco lo escobillo
Lo alegro lo baileo lo promuevo
Lo calmo lo sacudo lo patino
Lo alabo lo tonteo lo desquicio
Lo hincho lo reviento lo asesino
Lo curo lo alimento lo medico
Lo humillo lo critico lo lapido
Lo admiro lo engrandezco lo celebro
Lo adoro lo derrito lo recibo
Y así (con tantas cualidades)
Lo extraño lo atravieso no lo encuentro

(remake of Girondo) [*]

I smell it I scrutinize it I ponder it
I seek it I uncomb it I stir it up
I yank it out of the pillow I pursue it
I prick it I shock it I respect it
I weigh it I evaluate it I honor it
I applaud it I instruct it I enrapture it
I see it I mirror it I palpitate it
I salt it I penetrate it I digest it
I squeeze it I screw it on I hurt it
I listen to it I secure it I comfort it
I scrape it I dampen it I brush it
I make it happy I dance about it I promote it
I calm it I shake it I patinate it
I extol it I talk nonsense to it I unhinge it
I make it swell up I burst it I assassinate it
I heal it I feed it I medicate it
I humiliate it I criticize it I stone it
I admire it I magnify it I celebrate it
I adore it I melt it I receive it
And thus (with so many qualities)
I miss it I run it through I fail to find it

Huele el viento a espuma del Atlántico
La sombra se articula como un rumor extranjero
De campanadas al compás del río
Una extraña picazón le raspa los pies a la ciudad
El Ciego deambula
Preguntando por el otro es el tiempo de los Vientos Árticos
Y el Hada Cristalina que toca con su vara erecta
Cuanto en piedra en barro en polvo
Se le tiende y lame
Es el tiempo de la alfombra mágica del último rosal el que
      aún tiene
La yema relumbrante de las cortaduras
Las pasiones secretas y las interrumpidas
Las miradas profundas que por un instante
Arrojan su deseo por la lengua
Es el tiempo es el tiempo —*el Hada proclama*—
Pidiendo que le rasguen las propias vestiduras
Con las arañas de un pincel

Así
Mirábanle y mirábanse alterados
Cubierto el mundo de doradas hojas de crujidos
Y colas acolchadas reventando

En la punta las flores encarnadas
Y al centro las agujas retorciéndose

21

The wind smells of Atlantic foam
Shadow articulates itself like the alien whisper
Of bells to the river's rhythm
An odd itch rasps the city's feet
The Blind One wanders about
Asking for the other one now is the time of Arctic Winds
And the Crystal Fairy who conducts with her stiff wand
Whatever in stone in mud in dust
Offers itself to her and licks
Now is the time of the magic carpet of the last rosebush
    which still has
A fingertip glittering with cuts
Secret passions and interrupted ones
Deep gazes that for an instant
Cast forth their desire via the tongue
Now is the time now is the time—*proclaims the Fairy*—
Demanding that they tear up her own clothes
With the spider of a paintbrush

Thus
They look at him and look at themselves altered *
The world covered with gold leaves of rustled
And cushioned tails exploding

On the tip incarnate flowers
And at the center writhing needles

Escrito en el sofá queda Su Nombre:
Retama de cabellos esparcidos
Y pálida manchilla humedecida
No vuelan ya los gritos que impregnaban
Los bordes de la sala con el rayo
De un sol anaranjado y terco:
Nunca llegó a gozarse tanto
De usar tan sólo lengua y dientes:

Piérdase el bosque en la retama seca
Y vuélvase la nuez descascarada
Un solo aroma

Ejercicio tan mínimo y valioso
Que eleva más que brazos y centellas

22

Written on the sofa Her Name remains:
Genista of spread hair
And a damp pallid stain
The cries that impregnated the hall's borders
With an orange and stubborn
Sun ray no longer fly:
Never was there such enjoyment
From using only tongue and teeth:

Lose the woods in the dry genista
And transform the shelled walnut
Into a single fragrance

An exercise so minimal and valuable
Which raises more than arms and flashes

Con el grosor de la gota que se aplaza desde el techo
Con el aliento súbito del joven enamorado que ya no tiene nada
    que perder
Con ganas de subir las escaleras
Yo musitaba Su Nombre en la sombra
Le hacía espacio entre las hojas en el suelo
Formando barro, costras, avenidas
Que luego tenderían sus amarras sobre el puerto

Hasta aquí sólo las olas se bastaban para calmar las noches
    infinitas su aliento de ciruela su recuerdo
De líquidos viscosos emergiendo en el rocío de las flores:
Así sus aguas jugosas pegamentos de cera en las iglesias que nunca
    recorrieron los amantes
Y la condena eterna del deseo simulado como si nada pasara como
    si no fuera suficiente
La tristeza del mundo

Esos jugos impregnan el tiempo como el aire en el vacío
Las oficinas sacudidas por la ausencia de empleados los rojizos
Subterráneos al fondo de la plaza todos y cada uno de los cuadros
    que no llegó a pisar
Como una promesa sin eco en la que sólo el marinero herido vive
Por la fonda perdida

Y con el mismo dolor en que he crecido
Con el mismo silencio en que Le escribo

With the thickness of the drop that summons itself from the ceiling
With the sudden breath of the young lover who no longer has
    anything to lose
With a desire to descend the stairs
I mumbled Her Name in the shadow
Making room for it among the leaves on the ground
Forming mud, scabs, avenues
Which then toss its mooring lines onto the port

Until now only waves sufficed to calm the infinite nights their plum
    breath their memory
Of viscous liquids emerging from the dew of flowers:
Thus their juicy waters sticky with wax never visited by lovers
And the eternal condemnation of feigned desire as if nothing will
    happen as if the sadness of the world
Was not enough

These juices impregnate time like air in the void
Offices shaken by the absence of employees reddish
Subways at the base of the plaza all and each one of the pictures he
    did not trample
Like a promise without an echo in which only the wounded sailor lives
By the lost tavern

And with the same pain in which I have grown
With the same silence in which I write to Her

Si Le escribo es por poblar esta página en blanco
La proporción de orilla que nos toca después de la crecida
Llenarla de guijarros hasta verla crecer
Apurar sus líneas pese a la arena

Allí se erguía el tablado perfecto para la misa
Allí subía a sacrificarme
Con una sonrisa inversa arañando el pecho
Mientras con cara de diablo hundía la mano
En lo más genital de lo terrestre
Perdida en las tinieblas gozaba su hervor fragante
Veía subir sus ondas como una serpiente jaspeada
Me fundía con los dioses Era diosa
Que luego encontraba salpicada en las plantas
Bajo el fuego de la lluvia y de su aliento

Toxcatl me llamaba
Por ser la diosa del tiempo
Y mientras sacaba la piedra
Y el dolor me cruzaba y chillaba la sangre
Sólo hacía lo necesario
Antes de volver con la aburrida tribu
A cocinar huesillos y abrir perros

Pese a todo
Aún vengo en las mañanas a poblarlo

Si los tontos supieran
Esta parte del campo no le pertenece a nadie
Y así como la descubrimos
Nos la quitan

24

If I write to Him it is to populate this blank page
The proportion of the shore assigned to us after the freshet
To fill it with pebbles until we see it grow
To purify its lines in spite of the sand

There the perfect stage for the Mass was erected
There I climbed to sacrifice myself
With an inverted smile spidering my chest
While with the face of the devil he plunged his hand
Into what was most genital of the terrestrial *
Lost in darkness I enjoyed its fragrant boiling
I saw its waves rise like a mottled snake
I merged with the gods I Was a goddess
Who then was found splashed on the plants
Under the fire of the rain and his breath

They called me Toxcatl
Because I am the goddess of time
And while he pulled out the stone
And pain cut through me and my blood screamed
He was only doing what he had to do
Before returning to his boring tribe
To cook little bones and to open up dogs

In spite of everything
I still come in the morning to populate it

If the fools only knew
This part of the field belongs to no one
And just as we discovered it
They will take it from us

Aparecen las flores que soñaba la diosa en su lecho de rosa
El mundo flota en estas líneas en el viento
Oloroso y delgado como un trompo
Marcando la ruta de un mapa
En sus espaldas

Viento que recorres el paisaje en los días fríos
Guarda tu alforja de pana y trae una gota de agua:
Esputos marismas espumas
Coágulos de savia salpicones
De chasquidos y un ruido de piedras que se quiebran
Sobre la costa en llamas

Se levanta la diosa en su lecho de rosa un tremor de catarata
Se oye a lo lejos *(a lo lejos alguien canta)* a lo lejos
Nunca llegó el contorno en sábana de bata:

Un árbol mezquino la persecución de los caminos
Que no pasan por poblado alguno que no piensan en las plantas
Desgarrándose de vidrios

Pero las líneas quedan y la suavidad del mundo es apenas empujada
Por una vaga luz de estrellas muertas

25

The flowers that the goddess dreamed of appear on her rose bed
The world floats on these lines in the wind
Odiferous and delicate like a top
Marking the route of a map
On her back

Wind that crosses the landscape on cold days
Put away your corduroy knapsack and fetch a drop of water
Spittle salt marshes foam
Clots of splattered sap
Of snappings and the sound of stones breaking
On the coast in flames

The goddess rises from her rose bed a cataract tremor
Heard from far away *(far away someone sings)* far away *
Her outline in a bed-sheet dressing gown never arrived:

A wretched tree the prosecution of roads
That pass through no towns that never think about soles
Torn by window glass

But the lines stay and the suavity of the world is hardly pressured
By the vague light of dead stars

Han llovido gotas de silencio sobre el asfalto cansado
Una muesca se dibuja sobre ese cielo negro
Como el mar que se calma por encima y no duele
Las súbitas cuerdas que descienden le clavan
Agujas de palabras de tiempos antiguos
Mar de fondo   Fosa perfumada
Sobre tu falsa cabeza se deslizan
Borrones y mareas diminutas
Suelas gastadas y uñas curvas
Todas ellas no borran la oscuridad viviente
Los siglos que rodaron como cántaros
Y el centro de la tierra entre dos piernas
Súbitamente alegres
                       Como un animal marino
Baboso de tinta

Drops of silence have rained on the tired asphalt
A notch is sketched into the black sky
Like the sea that calms on the surface and does not ache
Abruptly descending ropes nail it
Needles of words from ancient times
Ground swell   Perfumed Deep
Over your false head slides
Blots and diminutive tides
None erase the living darkness
The centuries that rolled about like jugs
And the center of the earth between two legs
Suddenly happy
                          Like a sea animal
Slimy with ink

Luna Mama Killa amamanta estos versos con solicitud
Quieren pensar que por ellos vivirías pero Tú trasciendes
Esas fronteras minúsculas del tiempo
Y brillas Low
Killa como un solo Ojo gigantesco
Que alivia los senderos y previene los rasguños acaricia
El ensueño de tu Kolgar
Luna Mama Killa brilla Nueva por todo lo alto cayendo sobre la
    Tierra
Arremete contra los arrecifes esparce tu espuma por las calles
Arde sobre los buques luminosos

Asalta la ciudad
En Tu Nombre

27

Moon Mama KrazyOne suckle these lines with solicitude
They'd like to think that because of them you would live but You
    transcend
These miniscule frontiers of time
And shine Low
KrazyOne a single gigantic Eye
Lightening paths and preventing scratches caresses
The dream of your Skaffolding
Moon Mama KrazyOne shine New over all the high falling on
    Earth
Attack reefs scatter your foam through the streets
Blaze over glowing ships

Assault the city
In Your Name

28

Porque tienes el Nombre de muchas
Y la belleza de todas
La soledad de los barcos en la noche
La solidez del nácar cuando se traga su perla
Al fondo de ese embudo rueda hasta su origen
Buscando la Conca
Vidad de su infancia

Porque tienes el Nombre de muchas
Y la belleza de todas
Bendita Tú eres entre todas las mujeres
Bendita la marea que chorrea por el dedo
Y bendito el dibujo que por un segundo
                                        Te atrapa

En su Sakra Boccata

Because you hold the Name of many
And the beauty of all
The solitude of boats at night
The strength of nacre upon swallowing its pearl
At the bottom of that funnel it rolls unto its origin
Searching for the Conca
Vity of its childhood

Because you hold the Name of many
And the beauty of all
Blessed are You among all women
Blessed the tide that trickles onto the finger
And blessed the design that for an instant
Ensnares you

In its Sakra Boccata

Concerning the title of the poem, Mazzotti writes:

> *Sakra Boccata* is a title coined after words for 'sacred' and 'mouthful' in Spanish/Italian. The Italian 'boccata' also refers to strongly exhaled or foul breath. In Spanish, the equivalent would be 'bocanada,' a word that can be divided into 'boca' (mouth) and 'nada' (nothing), a metaphor for the impotence of written poetry facing the splendor of poetic reality.
>
> 'Sakra' also evokes the Quechuan 'saqra,' a mischievous demon. Thus *Sakra Boccata* can also be read as 'a mouthful from the Devil,' which can refer to cunnilingus.
>
> The divine breath that God breathed into matter as well as a sense of poetry as an art that creates life are also present in the title. These ideas are of medieval origin at a time when poetry was conceived as the Queen of Arts and Sciences, as it should be.

"lengua casta-i-llana," p. ix: also refers to "lengua castellana" or Castilian language.

"The amber goddess has arrived," p. 13: a reference to a book by the Peruvian poet Emilio Adolfo Westphalen, *Ha vuelto la diosa ambarina* (1984). For Westphalen, "the amber goddess" is poetry.

"Your Konch is that exquisite place," p. 15: the reader will notice that some words are written with a K instead of a C (e.g., Konch, LoKilla, Kolgar). Certain Peruvian writers in the 1980s employed this substitution as a way to challenge conventional orthographic rules and to stress the oral components of poems. A representative case: "Kloaka" (for "Cloaca," or Sewer), an anarchist group of poets who denounced the excesses of the dirty war and complicity of most intellectuals in it during that decade.

"Red Rum Red Rum," p. 15: "Murder" written backwards, a playful allusion to a scene in Stanley Kubrick's film *The Shining* (1980).

"the Virgin of Chapi," p. 15: the patron saint of the Peruvian city of Arequipa worshipped on May 1 of every year.

"I vie to revert," p. 17: a translation of the distorted phrase, "Vusco volver" from *Trilce IX* by César Vallejo.

"your Lemnian profile," p. 17: a reference to the island of Lemnos (*Argonautics*, Chant I), where women reigned and killed their lovers after mating.

"Andronican," p. 17: pertaining to Titus Andronicus, the cruel Roman general in Shakespeare's early tragedy of the same name.

"Of the bright day that conjugates," p. 17: a translation of a phrase from *Trilce II*.

"Under the double arches... pass on tiptoes," p. 17: a translation of two lines from *Trilce LXV*.

"Mussel because this mounting," p. 21: the word "mounting" to pick up alliteration with "Mussel," ("choro" in Spanish) and to render "chanto," based on the verb "chantar," Peruvian slang for "intercourse."

"LoKilla," p. 23: or Loquilla in conventional Spanish, also refers to "Ki-lla," Moon in Quechua, a meaning that the literal translation of "LoKilla" (LittleKrazyOne) cannot convey.

"Little caramel mouth silken cutis," p. 27: translation of a line from a popular Peruvian song "La flor de la canela."

"So much death and no power at all against life," p. 29: a play of words on a line by Vallejo from *España, aparte de mí este cáliz* (1939), "XII / Masa," "Tánto amor, y no poder nada contra la muerte!" ("So much love, and no power at all against death!")

"molluscle," p. 35: a word coined in English off "muscle" and "mollusk" to match the coined "molúsculo" (based on "músculo" and "molusco").

"Friar Gómez," p. 35: a fictional character who performed miracles (like turning a scorpion into a precious jewel) in Ricardo Palma's tradición, or historical short story, *El alacrán de Fray Gómez.*

"Saint Tiváñez," p. 35: a reference to Roger Santiváñez, a Peruvian poet of the 1980s generation, known for his maudit style.

"primordiac," p. 47: a neologism after "primordial" and "cardiac."

"As in chaos and the first confusion," p. 47: translation of a line in Chant I of Alonso de Ercilla's, "La Araucana" (1569).

"(remake of Girondo)," p. 49: a reference to Poem 12 of *Espantapajáros (al alcance de todos)*, 1932, by the Argentine poet Oliverio Girondo.

"They look at him and look at themselves altered," p. 51: translation of a line from *Cortés valeroso* (1590) by Lobo Lasso de la Vega.

"Into what was most genital of the terrestrial," p. 57: translation of a line from "Alturas de Machu Picchu," a long section of Pablo Neruda's epic *Canto general* (1950).

"(far away someone sings)," p. 59: translation of a line from Neruda's "Poema 20," from his *Viente poemas de amor y una canción desesperada* (1924).